PRISON GRADUATES

[ACQUIRED PRISON TRAUMATIC SYNDROME (A.P.T.S)]

(A DRAMA IN FOUR LEGS)

BY EFO KODJO MAWUGBE

*Winner of the 2009 BBC World Service/British Council
International Radio playwriting Competition,
English as a 2nd language*

AFRAM PUBLICATIONS (GHANA) LIMITED

Published by:
Afram Publications (Ghana) Limited
P. O. Box M18
Accra, Ghana

Tel: +233 3024 2561, +233 244314103
E-mail: publishing@aframpubghana.com
              sales@aframpubghana.com
Website: www.aframpubghana.com

© Efo Kodjo Mawugbe Foundation, 2015

First Published 2015

ISBN: 9964 70 538 7

Dedication

COMRADE KWESI PRATT JNR.

Acknowledgement

The first cast: Kenneth Fiati, Ebenezer Osae Aye, Saviour Ashiagbor, Kofi Boakye, Wakefield Ackuaku, and all members of Kokromoti Drama Group.

Paul Lemonye who brought us together and encouraged us that Publishing Efo's books will be the best thing that can happen.

The wife and children of EKM; Akweley, Mikafui, Sefakor, Edem, Eyram and Sitso.

The **Efo Kodjo Mawugbe Foundation** members for coming together to fight for Efo's plays to be published.
The Foundation wishes to thank those without whom this publication would not have been possible: Marion Nancarrow, BBC Radio Drama Executive Producer, His Excellency Frédéric Clavier, French Ambassador to Ghana (2012-2015), Paulo Pais, Director of the Institut Français of Ghana, Stéphanie Soléansky, Cultural Attaché, Esi Sutherland-Addy, and the Editorial team of Afram Publications.

The BBC Perspective

When the news reached me that Efo Kodjo Mawugbe had died, I could not believe it. How could such a huge presence not be with us any more? How could a man with such vision, insight, humour and humility not be there to continue to tell his story, to help others tell theirs and to help us all to better understand the world and our place within it?

Efo Kodjo Mawugbe was a man of great talent, phenomenal insight, wonderful humour and a huge heart. I first worked with him in 2007, when he was Artistic Director of the National Theatre of Ghana and had written the first and last scenes in an interlinked drama by playwrights across Africa for BBC World Drama, to mark 50 years of Independence. When the idea was mooted that we might come to Ghana to record these scenes if we could harness such a recording to a bigger project, Efo immediately helped rally writers and actors to come to workshops on writing and acting for radio. Efo's play was about a car which began its journey in 1957 with the words "Freedom & Justice for All" emblazoned on its side. When the car returned in 2007, battered and limping, the words had become simply "Free Juice For All". One of my happiest memories is of him performing in his own play, whilst 40 people who'd attended the workshops stayed on to record songs and give the rally cries of the people who wanted their free juice!

Efo continued to write for the BBC – winning the African Performance competition and, for the BBC World Service, writing a very funny play about a young Ghanaian man who refused to study – inspired by a photograph sent in by a listener.

Then in 2009, I was lucky enough to meet Efo again. This time, as our guest, since he had won the first prize for English as a 2nd language in the BBC World Service/British Council International Radio Playwriting Competition. This was "The Prison Graduates". Four men try to make their way in the world after their release from prison in Ghana. They explore their many options – only to choose the one that might have surprised them all. This was a surreal, post-colonial fable – a sort of Woza Albert! meets Samuel Beckett. The judging panel (which included playwright, actor and director Kwame Kwei-

Armah and actor Vincent Ebrahim) described the play as "imaginative, muscular and hysterically funny". Efo said that he felt he had a story to tell, of independent African countries misusing the opportunity given to them. Part of his prize was to come to London for the recording of the play. He'd never been to a radio recording before and he seemed to love every moment: he came to the recording and to the editing. He wanted to see everything he could, so that he could share what he had learned on his return. He was surprised by the physicality of the recording – that our cast (Daniel Francis, Mo Sesay, David Gyasi, Richard Pepple and Wale Ojo) threw themselves around the studio and, where the story demanded, at each other!

I will remember Efo's wonderful speech on the night of the prize-giving ceremony in Shakespeare's Globe Theatre on London's Southbank. He recalled his father telling him not to be a playwright and now he wished his father could be there to see him, in Shakespeare's Globe theatre, accepting his award. But more than that, Efo typically urged the BBC and the British Council to continue the competition for the next generation – something he was always passionate about.

Although Efo used a pseudonym when he sent in his plays (a woman's name) because he knew that I was involved, it didn't work! I could always tell a play written by Efo: it would be insightful, side-splittingly funny, but sharp and always with a vision of the world and of what needed to change. The judges described him as a Ghanaian Samuel Beckett.

Efo taught me so much. He loved his country and its people and cared passionately about both. He and his characters made me laugh and sometimes made me cry. I miss him on a personal as well as a professional level, but his passion for telling stories and revealing truths and for encouraging successive generations of talent will continue to inspire.

Marion Nancarrow
Executive Producer, BBC Radio Drama, London

CHARACTERS

Apart from the Chaplain and the man who appears in a tuxedo at the end of the play, all four major characters are ex-convicts just released from the local Maximum Security Prison.

Abutu: A very hot-tempered young man.
              Doubles as "Nurse II" and "Orderly".

Chaka: Leader of the group. Doubles as
              "Nurse I" and "Abusua Panyin".

Basabasa: Speaks Pidgin English with amazing
              fluency.

Gomido: Hot-blooded and never sees eye to eye with
              Abutu.

Prison Officer: Doubles as Chaplain & Voice.

1

.... **LEG 1** ....

[Sound of distant church bell. A distant Lone voice reciting what sounds like a remixed version of Psalm 23.]

Lone Voice: The Lord is our shepherd, We shall not want. He maketh us to lie down on cold dungeon floors... He locketh us behind the steel bars and says He restoreth our self esteem...

[Heavy crunching footsteps as in military Boots.]

More Voices: Yea though we live through this valley of our prison sentences, we'll fear no prison officer, for thou art with us. Thy rod and thy staff...

[Sound of very heavy iron gatesopening.]

Prison Officer: Order. . . Order! I say!
                        [*There is instant silence.*]

[Heavy military footsteps.]

P. Officer:	[*Clears his throat.*] The following inmates have been granted presidential amnesty and are to be released unconditionally. They are therefore to proceed to the Chaplain's office for their discharge papers and other documents. They are... [*Pause. Clears throat*] Prisoner number... xyz24.
Abutu:	Yes, Sir!
P. Officer:	Prisoner number www. 96.
Gomido:	Yes, Sah!
P. Officer:	[*Talking very fast*] Prisoner number PT 007.
Chaka:	Yes, Sir!
P. Officer:	[*Talking really fast*] Prisoner KW.66
Basabasa:	Hallelujah!
All Inmates:	AMEN!
P. Officer:	Who is that dozing prisoner? [*Pause*] Since when did Hallelujah and its next door neighbour, Amen, become the standard prison call and response?
Basabasa:	I sorry Sah. . . Na slip of tongue Sah!

P. Officer: Slip of brain more likely. Four of you are to come along with me to the chaplaincy. Orderly!

Orderly: Yes Sah!

P. Officer: Take them to the Chaplain's office for their belongings and discharge papers.

Orderly: Yes Sah! Permission to carry on Sah!

Officer: Carry on.

Orderly: [*Issuing out orders*] Prisoners, about turn. By the left, quick march, left-right, left-right, left-right… Left-right…left-right… (*singing freedom freedom everywhere here must be freedom*)

[Marching footsteps going.]

[Christian hymn. A deep voice humming along the hymn.]

Chaplain: In the name of the Father, the Son and the Holy Ghost… Amen!

Prisoners: Amen!

Chaplain: You are now free, liberated in fact, emancipated!

Abutu: And emaciated!

Chaplain: Well, Number 24, you can't blame me.
            Mine was to feed you spiritually which
            i believe i did to the best of my ability.
            [*he goes round shaking their hands*] The
            almighty lord in heaven that paseeth all
            understanding be and abide with you ....

Gomido: [*In a sudden outburst.*] Blast your hand
            shake Reverend... I'd rather shake hands
            with a leper than with a double-tongued
            charlatan.

Basabasa: Ma bruda, 96, wetin be de wahala? Beg
            your pardon.

Chaka: Those are very strong words to use against
            a Man of God.

Abutu: Such words could easily earn you a free
            multiple visa to hell.

Gomido: [Removes his trousers and bends down
            to face chappie] Osofo this is my assport
            stamp the multiple entry visa in thereYou
            hypocrite, You Serpent!

Chaka: Number 96, Stop it.

Chaplain: [*Not in the least ruffled. Coolly sings along the
            hymn in the background*] May the good Lord
            of Heaven, have mercy on you my boy.

Gomido: And may the same Lord delete your name
              from the register of His good shepherds.

Basabasa: Oh No! 96, why you de block una chance
                to enter heaven?

Gomido: Don't you worry, by the time we get to
              heaven… that is if there is any such place,
              this wolf in sheep's clothing would be
              nowhere there.

Chaka: Cease fire!
              [*Silence*]

Chaplain: Well, I think you ought to be going now.

Abutu, Chaka: Yes, Chappie… Bye, Chappie.
  & Basa

Chaplain: Bye, and may the good Lord be with you,
              24, 007, and 66… and the devil with that
              one over there . . .

[Loud shutting of door.]

Gomido: You heard him, didn't you? I tell you, folks,
              if that Chappie were God's tap-turner,
              he'd ensure water flows only to his
              mother-in-law's kitchen.

Chaka: Come on, Let us forget about him.

Gomido: You can forget, but not I who bear the
            scar of his treachery.

Abutu: Why all this deep bitterness towards the
            Man of God?

Gomido: Hmmm . . . I had to do a time-added on,
            all because of him.

Abutu: Time-added-on... When?

Gomido: He was the Chaplain at Anomabo Prison
            where I began to serve my sentence. By
            then I had become a born-again Christian.
Chaka: You say you had become what-again?

Gomido: Born-Again!

            [*Laughter from colleagues*]

Basa: Let us all pray... "Our farda, which art in
            Heaven, make una forget our daily bread
            as we already de steal from bakers dat
            don't trespass against us"... Wonders
            never go end. A cockroach becoming
            born-again?

Gomido: Believe me, folks. In prison I lift up both
            hands in full surrender and accepted Jesus
            Christ as my Lord and personal Cellmate.
            [*Chaka and the rest break into laughter*]
            Chappie said the Lord, My Lord was ever
            faithful and just to forgive us all of our

7

sins, transgressions and iniquities.

Abutu: Oh yes, and *"He could turn your scarlet red sins into snow white bed sheets. . . ."*

Gomido: Those were his exact words. Did he play the same trick on you?

Abutu: Not me, but on Tsatsu, a very good friend of mine, at Nsawam Prison.

Chaka: And what happened?

Gomido: Hmmm. . . I was so moved by Chappie's sermon that day, I went up to him after the church service. [*Sob*]

Gomido: [*Sob*] To confess a robbery I was involved in …but had until then not been detected by the police. [*Sob*]

Chaka: You did what?

           [*There is a long silence.*]

Abutu: What happened after that?

Gomido: The following morning, I was re-interrogated and whisked to court…[*sob*]… tried…and sentenced to do three years of time- added- on. [*Sob*]

Chaka & Co: Oh No!

Basabasa: Abi, you craze?... Beg your pardon.

Abutu: The Chappie outsmarted you.

Gomido: [*Sob*] I never knew that every Prison
              Chappie worked for God above and the
              system below. [*Sob*]

Basabasa: My brudas, if una look-look de matter
              proper-proper, I tink say, technically
              speaking, we no for put blame on Chappie.

Chaka & Co: Why?

Basabasa: De Chappie him never say if una confess
              una CRIME, de state or de law of de land
              go forgive una. Chappie say dat, de Lord
              which art in Heaven, hallowed be thy
              name ...na him go forgive una SINS.

Abutu: You are right. Technically speaking, a sin
              may not necessarily be a crime in the eyes
              of the law of the land.

Basa: Na so!... Beg your pardon.

Chaka: In other words, whereas the Lord which
              art in Heaven shall always forgive us our
              sins, when we confess them, the law of the
              land shall punish us for the crimes we
              confess.

Basa: Na so.

Gomido: [*Almost to himself*] So, there was a catch.
             [*Gomido sobs*]

Chaka: Stop crying. All that belongs to the past
             now. My brother, wipe your tears. Let's
             talk about something else.

Abutu: Something else, such as…?

Basa: Such as Freedom, what else.

Chaka: I tell you folks, the only time you experience
             the beauty of democracy is when you step
             out of prison after a long sentence.

Abutu: Sure, no one understands freedom better
             than a prisoner

Basa: Like Kwame Nkrumah!

Gomido: Like Nelson Mandela! [*Sings*] Free.. . Nelson
             Mandela, walking side by side with
             Winnie Mandela. . . on the crowded
             narrow streets of SOWETO.

Abutu: Can you imagine you are in this prison...
             For so many years…. Then, one day, out
             of the blue, you have all the freedom in
             the world hurled at you…in fact, thrown
             at you.

Chaka: Like a basketball?

Gomido: A basketball can hurt your fingers if you
             don't know how to handle it.

Chaka: That may be true, my brother, but I feel
             freedom ought not be looked at as an
             abstract concept.

Gomido: I agree freedom is never more sharply
             focused than when it is denied to you. But
             it could equally be dangerous when
             thrown at you like a basketball.

Basa: For me, ino dey like basketball at all.

Abutu &
Chaka: How does it make you feel?

Basa: I feel say make I shout Freedom!...
             Freedom!... Free…
             [Laughter]

Chaka: What about you, 24?

Gomido: *[As if reciting a poem]* I feel like sleeping
             and dreaming. Dreaming unfettered
             dream of all prison inmates, Joining
             hands and chanting songs of Asafo And

11

driving out all the prison officers And
taking over the prisons.

**[A Fiery Asafo War Song. Ex-Convicts Join in
the Singing.]**

A dream of a prison without walls…
And without cheating prison officers…

Abutu: Hold it there! [*Pause*]
Inmate 96, you are under arrest!

Gomido: Where is my crime?

Abutu: Your crime is in your head.

Gomido: What?

Abutu: You are under arrest for attempting to
sleep and dream. And dreaming and
preaching anarchy and mutiny in your
dream. [*Gomido tries to explain*] You have
every right to remain silent. Any thing
you say here and now may be used
against you in a court of law in
dreamland.[*Pause*]. Meanwhile you are
hereby sentenced to…[*pause*]
Your freedom! [*Laughter*]

Chaka: [*To Abutu*] And you, 24, tell us how
you feel right now.

Abutu:	To tell you the truth, I feel like a nation having just attained independence after centuries of colonial rule.
Basa:	Na true. So make we change una names. Beg your pardon. [*Pause*]
Gomido:	007, I think the brother is right. We need new names and a new freedom song. A national anthem. [*He begins to sing "God save the Queen"*]
Basa:	Abi wey kine funeral song be dat one?
Gomido:	That is our new national anthem. Don't you like it?
Abutu:	No!
Chaka:	Why?
Abutu:	We need to be original. We need something of our own. To reflect our new status… Our sovereignty… We need to create for ourselves a new identity… A new personality A new flag …
Basa:	Na so, a new brand of freedom flag!
Gomido:	Remember former Tanganyika…

former Northern and Southern Rhodesia…

Abutu: South West Africa…
               The Gold Coast…
               Dahomey…

Chaka: That is definitely better than referring to
               each other by the numbers given to us
               from our prison past.

Abutu & Co: Precisely.

Chaka: So, you, Number 24, what shall be your
               new name?

Abutu: I want to be known as AYITEY
               HEWALE. Alias ABUTU.

Chaka: And you, my Bruda, Number 96?

Gomido: I wish to be called YAOVI NUNYA a.k.a.
               GOMIDO!

Chaka: [*To BASABASA.*] What about you
               number 66?

Basabasa: [*As if he is a child reciting a nursery rhyme.*]
               De title of my new name na "BASA-into-
               Brackets-Squared." [*ABUTU bursts out
               laughing*] Even though the name my mama
               den papa give me for baby na Shika.
               Wetin, my name no sweet?
               Beg your pardon.

Abutu: Come to think of it. . . an illiterate rural Primary School dropout, having for his name a mathematical equation. [*Laughs*]

Basa: Your morda be de Rural… Your farda be de rural.   Your. . .

Chaka: Cease fire!

[*Silence*]

Abutu: Well.

Gomido: Well, what?

Abutu: [*To Chaka*] 007, I think it is your turn to let us know your Independence name.

Chaka: Well, I used to be number 007. For now, I wish to be known and called Nana… Akwasi…Timber aka Chaka!

Abutu: Chakaaaa!...Chakaaaa! Chak…

Gomido: Hey…hey… Will you stop shouting.

Abutu: Can't a man exercise his freedom to shout? Why do you want to make me feel as if I am still in prison? By the way, who made you a Prison Officer over me?

Gomido: No one here says you can't shout. What

	you need to know is, your shouting must end where the other fellow's ear begins.
Basa:	Na true.
Abutu:	That's nonsense. It is most undemocratic. If I should end my shouting just where the other fellow's ears begin, what guarantee is there that he has heard me?
Basa:	Abi, you craze? Or una get alligator pepper for u nash. Una want de eardrums break Poooaaah! before you sabey say him fit to hear you?
Abutu:	Will you shut up!
Basa:	I no go shut up.
Abutu:	Of course I don't blame you. You are an illiterate rural beg-your-pardon-nobody so…
Gomido:	Oh no! Not again
Basa:	Tank you, Me, I sabey say, I no go sukulu before.
Abutu:	You unpolished illiterate Rat.
Chaka:	Will you stop what you are doing?

Basa: Me, I be Rat ino be so? You be so foolish
          say, like you be goat wey dem kill you
          make pepper-soup and fufu, I swear, I
          go eat my fufu raw, I no go touch you
          self!

Chaka: Stop it, I say. [*Silence*] All this post-inde-
          pendence name-calling and undermining
          won't take us anywhere. It is most
          unhealthy for our post-prison life. We are
          a free people. What we do with our newly
          found freedom should be our major
          concern. Our collective future as brand
          new ex-convicts is what should engage
          every ounce of energy left in us. Do you
          understand?

Gomido: Well-spoken Chaka.

Basa: So, de question be say, wetin man for do
          for life outsai prison, ino be so?

Chaka: Exactly. What do we do, now that we are
          free?

Gomido: That question, I believe, goes to all of us.

          [*Breaks into a popular tune "Now That
          we've found love what are we gonna do
          with it?" All the others join in singing the
          first few bars in acapella fashion*]

Abutu: I tell you guys, I wish to go into management.

	I mean to manage boxers and footballers.
Gomido:	Any previous skills in that discipline?
Abutu:	There's no need for that. Particularly on this south side of the Sahara.
Basa:	Football na leda, boxing gloves na leda. But why una want to put money for inside leda?
Abutu:	Show me any durable purse that is not made of leather. Besides, most of our foot-ballers and boxers are highly talented ... but, [*Whispers*] very often, stark illiterate.
Chaka:	So, you intend to exploit their illiteracy, I guess.
Abutu:	That's most unfair! I am a businessman. All I do is scout for buyers on the foreign market and sell out the local boys. If I sell a player for 150,000 US Dollars, I pay the player 15,000 Dollars.
Gomido:	That's business.
Abutu:	Thank you, my brother.
Gomido:	A very crooked business at that.
Abutu:	Nonsense.

Basa: As for me, whether ibi nonsense or no
             nonsense, de tin wey I wan sabey be say,
             which sai una for ged de boxers?

Abutu: Right here. Gomido and Basabasa here,
             will do the fighting, with you Chaka as
             the sole-referee-judge, whilst I manage
             them. [*To Basa & Gomido*] They fight
             twice a year and earn five million cedis
             per fight for the next ten years. How
             about that?

[Takes a sheet of paper from his bag.]

Abutu: Please just sign on this dotted line.

Gomido: What's the paper for?

Abutu: Standard Contract. That ensures you
             belong to my stable.

Basa: Beg your pardon! ...A stable? Who talk
             you say I want to make horse my room-
             mate? [*General laughter*] Make you plus
             your contract go quench for sea.

Abutu: And you, Gomido?

Gomido: That's not the kind of fight I am interested
             in. I want to fight Satan from the pulpit.

Basa & Co: Beg your pardon.

Gomido:	I'll establish a synagogue.
Basa:	Hallelujah!
Chaka & Co:	Amen!
Basa:	Abi wetin name na your... errmmm… errmmm… Sy…na… sy na… what?
Gomido:	Synagogue of Jesus Christ of the people, by the people and for the people.
Chaka:	The first Global Democratic Church of Christ. Let's all say Amen to that.
Basa & Co:	Amen!

[Praise session in a typical charismatic church]

Gomido:	[*Sings as a soloist*] Darling Jesus, Democratic Jesus *Oh democratic Jesus you are wonderful Lord!* *I love you so, democratic Jesus* *Oh my Darling Jesus you are democratic Lord!* *Amen!*

[Loud applause of church congregation]

Abutu:	Announcements please. [*Pause*] The congregation is reminded that there shall be a ten–day Holy Spirit Revival/Crusade

from 8.30 am to 6.00pm everyday begin-
ning from tomorrow. All church members
must make it a point to attend. End of
announcement Amen!

Chaka: Now is the time to hear the word of God.
            There is a man right here on whose tongue
            the Lord Himself has placed healing
            words of honey for His children, Amen!

Abutu & Co: Amen!

Chaka: If you agree with me let's give a great
            shout to the Lord as we welcome…

Basa: De Honourable…Most Holy…Very
            Reverend…Bishop…Pastor…
            Evangelist…Prophet…Doctor…
            Gomey!

Abutu & Co: Amen!

Gomey: Praise the Lord!

Basa & Co: Hallelujah!

Gomey: [*Assumes the role of a charismatic Preacher*]
            The good book teaches us to lay up our
            treasures where?

Chaka & Co: In Heaven!

Gomey: Yes, But you can only get there through
                your Bishop. Your Bishop, is God's own
                chosen gatekeeper to the divine treasure
                throve of Heaven. So, channel all your
                treasures here on earth through, who?

Chaka & Co: THE BISHOP!

Gomey: I say through who?

Chaka & Co: The BISHOP!

Gomey: Yes, …If you want God to grant you
                prosperity in life, make sure you don't
                miss the coming ten-day power-packed
                Holy Spirit-filled Crusade. Some of you
                might be saying the time conflicts with
                your work. Tell me, which is more
                important, God's work or man's work?

Basa & Co: God's work!

Gomey: If your work is going to bother you, just
                report sick at the hospital. Ask the Doctor
                to give you five days sick–off. After the
                fifth day you go back for a review and
                request for additional five days or ask for
                a ten-day casual leave from your
                employers. Amen!

Abutu & Co: Amen!

Chaka: No wonder productivity is so low.

Gomey: To tell you the truth, all I really want to do is to go into farming.

Abutu & Co: Farming! Are you crazy?

Chaka: Why choose such a backbreaking labour-intensive occupation?

Abutu: May be he intends going into mechanized farming: tractors, combine harvesters and all that.

Gomey: Well, may be.

Basa: Beg your pardon, Wey kine crop you go plant, pineapples?

Gomey: Nah!

Chaka: Cocoa

Gomey: Naah!

Chaka: Sugarcane production then?

Gomey: There's more money in my type of special "cane" crop than in sugarcane.

Abutu & Co: Prove it.

Gomey: Sugarcane, for example is harvested…

Chaka: Refined and packaged...

Abutu: Shipped, marketed and ...

Basa: Dem sell am for supermarkets at...

Abutu & Co: One dollar or one dollar fifty cents per kilo.

Gomey: Excellent. My special Cane crop goes through the same process of harvesting, refining, packaging, shipping, marketing and finally retailing.

Abutu & Co: Oh, I see!

Gomey: Wholesale price is between thirty to thirty five thousand US Dollars a kilo.

Abutu & Co: Whew! That is money!

Gomey: So, you see, given a choice, and the rudimentary knowledge of simple arithmetic, why would anyone in their right mind want to be in the sugar cane business?

Chaka: You still haven't mentioned the name of the crop.

Gomey: Come round let me tell you.
                (*Pause*)

Abutu & Co: Cocaine!

Chaka:	Arrest him!
	(*There is long silence.*)
Chaka:	(To Gomey) Tell me, where did you get that idea?
Gom& Co:	Jeffery Robinson, The Laundryman, page 171, at the prison library. [*They all break into laughter.*]
Abutu:	Folks, I am off.
Chaka:	Where does he think he is going?
Abutu:	I won't be staying in this bishop-corrupted, cocaine-juiced and God-forsaken country Southside of the vast Sahara for one more day. I am going away.
Gomido:	Away, to where?
Abutu:	I am going abroad!
Gomido:	Abroad, where?
Basa:	Lagos, in Nigeria? (*Silence*)
Abutu:	To Europe.
Chaka:	Do you have a passport?

Abutu: That's no problem. See this?

Chaka: What about this?

[Shows him about four sheets of paper stapled]

Basa: Wetin be dat?

Chaka: Visa Application forms.

Abutu: May I have a look?

Chaka: Here, BASA, pass them over to him.

[Abutu goes through the sheets]

Abutu: What! Am I expected to answer all that?

Gomido: If you really want me to consider you for an interview to determine your face qualifies for an entry visa to Europe. [*Assumes the role of a female consular officer interviewing applicants for visa.*]

Gomido: Youngman.

Basa: Yes, Madam,

Gomido: You take this slip and come back at 1.30pm for your visa

Basa: Thank you, Madam..

Gomido: [*Speaking with a false cockney accent. He pronounces the name as if he were a European being confronted with an African name for the first time.*]
Francis Kokosiko Abutu, interview room number eight please... [*Pause*] ...
Francis Kokosiko Abutu, Interview Room eight, please.

Abutu: Good morning, Madam!

Gomido: Good morning, you may sit.

Abutu: Thank you. But I prefer to stand.

Gomido: As you wish, may I have your documents.

Gomido: Your full name!

Abutu: Pardon me!

Gomido: Your name... full name,

Abutu: Abutu, Ayitey-Hewale. Kokosiko

Gomido: Date of birth.

Abutu: 31st February 1936

Gomido: Place of birth.

Abutu:	From Bukom, Accra.
Gomido:	Time of birth, if known,
Abutu:	Not applicable.
Gomido:	Mother's Name.
Abutu:	Naa Amanua Gborbilorbi.
Gomido:	Mother's place of birth.
Abutu:	Amasaman.
Gomido:	Mother's date of birth.
Abutu:	Ermm. . .errmm . . . No idea.
Gomido:	Father's name.
Abutu:	Nii Kwartei Quartey alias Nokoko.
Gomido:	Father's date and place of birth.
Abutu:	Swalaba-Accra, but no idea about date.
Gomido:	Parents' profession.
Abutu:	Father is a fisherman. Mother is a fish seller.
Gomido:	Monthly salary of father. (*Pause*) Yes, your father's monthly salary.

Abutu:	Eeerrrmm. . . No idea… I mean not applicable.
Gomido:	[*Sips coffee from a nearby cup*] Siblings… [*Pause*]… I mean number of Brothers and Sisters.
Abutu:	Oh that…I see, I have five brothers and three sisters.
Gomido:	Names of brothers...
Abutu:	Kpakpo, Nii Moolai, Ashong, Akwei and Papa Nii.
Gomido:	Sisters…
Abutu:	Ayorkor, Atswei and Naa Adaku.
Gomido:	Married or not married?
Abutu:	Mmm… Well… some are married, others divorced… others too have remarried and separated…or are on the verge of getting separated.
Gomido:	Do you have any family members living in Europe?
Abutu:	My family member? … My family … I don't get you…
Gomido:	By a 'family member', I am referring to

> your Spouse, Father, Mother, Son,
> Daughter, Great Grandfather, Great
> Grand-mother, Niece or First Cousin...

Abutu: First Cousin?

Gomido: The Son or Daughter or your Uncle or Aunt.

Abutu: I see, now I understand

Gomido: Good, so, back to my question. Do you
            have any family members living in
            Europe?

Abutu: Yes, and by your definition, all members
            of the West Indian community in the UK
            are my family members.

Gomido: What! ... [*Pause*] Now, are you married?

Abutu: Yes, Madam

Gomido: Name of wife

Abutu: Gbeebi Akley

Gomido: Was it church wedding or...

Abutu: Customary wedding.

Gomido: Date and Place of wedding.

Abutu: 24th December, at Kaadjaanor.

Gomido: Let me see your left hand.... Why no ring
            on your finger?

Abutu: In customary marriage, we bear the oath
            of marriage on our hearts, where it is
            sealed in blood and flesh by our total
            respect for our wives and their love for us.

Gomido: That's interesting. What is your
            profession?

Abutu: I am a Barrister.

Gomido: I see. Any letter of Support?

Abutu: Here you are.

            [Rustling of papers]

Gomido: I see…So you are a solicitor

Abutu: Excuse me.

Gomido: Which Law firm do you work for?

Abutu: Me… Law firm? I say I work with a bar…
            Chop Bar… Drinking Bar!

Gomido: What guarantee, is there that you will
            come back when you are given the visa to
            enter Europe? [*Pause*] Any property?

Abutu: I don't get you?

Gomido: Any possessions of value?

Abutu: Oh yes. I have three cats, two dogs, one cutlass, and one cocoa-spraying machine still under repairs with the mechanic: A pair of rain boots and a sizeable cassava farm cultivated under the Presidential Special Cassava Initiative.

Gomido: Is that all?

Abutu: I also have my pregnant wife.

Gomido: I see. Letter of invitation.

Abutu: It is among the documents I gave you [*Pause*]

Gomido: Yes, indeed, it is here. Reason for seeking visa… VISIT.

Abutu: That's right.

Gomido: Supposing you are offered a job in Europe during your visit, won't you take it?

Abutu: A job that pays well?

Gomido: A job that pays more than what you are receiving here. Euro or Pounds… Sterling! Let's say 950.00 Euro a week.

Abutu: Mmmm…well… That's a handsome
            amount of money compared to what one
            can have here…950.00 Euro a week…
            Wow! Who'll offer me a thing like that?

Gomido: A company.

Abutu: An European company?

Gomido: You bet.

Abutu: I am afraid, I'll turn it down.

Gomido: Why?

Abutu: Those people never offer anything for
            free. There's always some hidden string
            attached somewhere.

Gomido: Well, I am sorry, by the look in your eyes
            and the shape of your nose, I feel convinced
            you are not the type who'll return to this
            country if you ever stepped in Europe. So,
            I am denying you the visa. Here, take
            your passport.

Abutu: Then give me back my money… No
            delivery, no payment.

Chaka: What is he saying?

Basa: Him money. Beg your pardon. In dis

	country, No delivery-No payment. Him want him money.
Gomido:	No way. It is non-refundable. He can make an appeal.
Chaka:	An appeal will take Six months, Madam.
Gomido:	Six months it will take and what of that? Good afternoon gentleman.
Abutu:	I don't want to appeal. Give me back my money. Hey you, I am talking to you. Give me back my money.
Basa:	My bruda, dem close. Madam don go for lunch.
Abutu:	Cheats! You knew you were not going to issue me with the visa, and yet you deliberately subjected me to a humiliating interrogation as if I were a criminal under cross-examination in a court of law. Is that how you were interviewed at our national Mission in your country when you went seeking a visa to come down here? Give me back my money! Where in your country is a man paid ¢900,000.00 for interviewing a person for less than fifteen minutes?
Basa:	Abi, dis place na foreign embassy. Make una talk diplomatically.

Abutu: What has been done to me is pure diplomatic extortion. They are all Diplomatic robbers. You are all a bunch of Diplomatic extortionists… Hoo! Ole! Jaguda! Ewi… Julor kwakwe! Hoo!…

[Classical Music.]

[Silence]

Abutu: *[Very solemnly]* Nine Hundred and Ninety Thousand whole Cedis gone down the drain.

Chaka: *[Softly]* Five Hundred young people from this land of poverty apply for Visa and are denied everyday . . .

Basa: Make we times 500 by ¢990,000.00

Gomido: ¢495,000,000.00

Abutu: Multiply that by Monday, Tuesday, Wednesday, Thursday and Friday

Basa: Five days in a week.

Gomido: That gives you Two Billion Four hundred and Seventy Five Million Cedis only. (¢2,475,000,000.00).

Chaka: Again multiply that by the four weeks in a month! *[Pause]*.

Gomido:	¢9.9billion
Abutu:	Multiply by twelve months in a year. [*Pause*]
Gomido:	¢188.8billion… Oh my God! That can pay for over 500 bore holes to provide potable water for our rural folks in 300 villages… and re-gravel several kilometres of feeder road…
Basa:	Beg your pardon. . . It fit to construct proper classroom blocks for 250 rural communities to save our teachers from holding classes under trees!
Abutu:	That is the unsolicited contribution by our poor folks from this God forsaken side of the Atlantic Ocean, to the economy of former colonial masters. [*Chaka suddenly bursts out into laughter. He is unable to control his laughter*]
Gomido:	What's funny? … [*Chaka, still laughing*]
Chaka:	For all you know, it is that money they turn round to give us as medium term loan for development
Basa:	Yes! Na true! Na true talk . . . Ibi de same money!
Chaka & Co:	Hey! Sh-sh-sh-sh. Not so loud. Walls

have ears!
[*Silence*]

Gomido: To be honest with you, what I really want
           to be is a Professor of politics. Stand for
           elections, go to parliament and fight for
           human rights. [*General laughter*]

Basa: Who talk you say de hungry people for dis
           land dem want vote for somebody wey
           him ged prison record?

Gomido: You never entered a classroom, so you
           know nothing about history.

Chaka: What has history got to do with this?

Basa: Make una hask am now

Gomido: Everything.

Abutu: Such as?

Gomido: Joseph came out of prison to be the Prime
           minister to the Pharaoh of Egypt. That's
           number one.

Chaka: Oh…I see, Chappie really did a thorough
           job on you. Why don't you rather be a
           preacher man? [Laughter] On a more
           serious note, after Joseph who came?

Basa: I tink say after Joseph de next one go be

Mary, Jesus him morda. [*Laughter*]

Gomido: You are wrong. Rather it was Malcolm X. An African-American who came out of prison to give racist America of his time, a piece of mirror to take a good look at her conscience. That's number two.

Chaka: And number three?

Gomido: Abdel Gamal Nasser, came out of prison to lead Egypt…Number four, Dr. Kwame Nkrumah, The Osagyefo himself, came out of prison to lead the Gold Coast into Ghana.

Chaka: That's true.

Basa &Abutu: And number five?

Gomido: Nelson Mandela! Landed by helicopter from Roben Island to lead the ANC and South Africa through the narrow streets of SOWETO into freedom's highway singing *Nkosi kele le Africa!. Malufaka yiso opondola yo!.*

[*They all join in singing the Anthem up to a point.*]

Chaka: Okay…Okay! Any more?

Gomido: Just two and I will be done. In neigh-bouring Nigeria, Moshood Abiola nearly came out of prison to lead that country. And in Ghana, a certain Jerry John Rawl…

Abutu: Objection! [*Pause*] Strictly speaking folks, that chap was in an army guardroom and not a real prison like you and I have been through.

Basa: Him too ino be thief like me plus you.

Gomido: Don't tell me what you don't know. That chap was a common criminal just like any of us here. He was arrested attempting to steal.

Basa: Wetin him go tief? Beg your pardon.

Gomido: Political power.

Chaka: I think, what you want us to understand is that, you are a potential parliamentary material, in spite of your Ex-Con record.

Gomido: Precisely, and more so when I am now a Born-Again Christian.
            [*The rest burst out into laughter*]

Chaka: So, you want to become a Parliamentarian.

Gomido: That's right! A Senator.

Chaka: All right. Now, we invite our aspiring Born-Again Senator to address members

of his constituency herein assembled.
Silence everybody! [*Pause*]

Gomido: I don't seem to get you.

Chaka: You may mount the podium over there.
             You have two and a half minutes to
             address us on our present circumstances.
             Energy crisis, The Leopard called NEPAD,
             Indiscipline, corruption in the judiciary,
             The Presidential Special Gutter Cleaning
             Initiative, the depreciating currency, HIPC
             and all. You may begin at the sound of the
             whistle. I shall be the timekeeper. You,
             BASABASA, will be my clock. At the
             sound of the whistle, begin ticking.

Gomido: Wait a minute… you mean I should…

[Sound of a Whistle]

Gomido: You mean I should pretend this is some
             real political rally and . . .

Basa: Ke..ke..ke..ke…ke…ke. Half a minute
             gone! Ke…ke..ke..ke..ke..ke.

Gomido: [*Suddenly realises the full importance of the
             game.*] Tsooooboee!… [*No response*]
             Tsoooooboe! [*No response.*]

Abutu: Ke…ke…ke...ke…ke… Another half a

minute gone.

Gomido: [To no one in particular] What do I do
now? [*Clears his throat*] My people, do
not fear circumstances. They cannot hurt
us. It is not the circumstances in which
we are placed that matters. It is not the
circumstances enforced on us by the
energy crisis that matters… But the spirit
in which we as a nation, and as a people,
meet them, as challenges, that constitutes
our comfort. Above all, I want you to
believe that there's NOTHING you
cannot accomplish as a people by hard
work and commitment. Therefore, let NO
ONE, be he or she in or outside
Government ever destroy that belief you
have in yourself as a people. Say to
yourselves "Yes we can" Thank you.

Basa: Time Up!

[Long sound of whistle]

Chaka: So far, so good. Can we have the first
question please? Yes, you young man at
the back there.

Basa: [*With South African accent*] Thank you,
Mr. Moderator. Lucky Mphalele is
my name and I represent the Sowetan, a
community newspaper produced in

41

South Africa . Please Mr. Aspiring
Senator, what in your opinion, do you
think, is the cause for democracy being
unable to thrive for long on the sub-Saharan
political soil?

Gomido: Is that an optional question?

Abutu: [*Angrily*] What a question. Don't you
know that in every examination, the
Question One is compulsory? Go check
from the West African Exams Council.

Gomido: Thank you. The truth of the matter
is that democracy is not a feasible
proposition within any nation that is
plagued by deprivation and grinding
poverty. Sub-Saharan Africa remains the
zone of the most desperate suffering in the
post-cold war world. The answer to its
multiple problems does not lie simply in
good governance, or observance of human
rights or positive defiance. It lies more in
the developed world's response to Africa's
genuine developmental needs.
Sub-Saharan Africa's crisis is not an
isolated issue. We must see it as the world's
crisis.

Abutu: [**Speaks with an American accent**] Well
said, I am Joe Bush of the International
Enquirer based in London. Must
Sub-Saharan Africa wait perpetually for

the slumbering Developed World to wake up whilst its children die by the hordes everyday?

Gomido: No.

Abutu: If no, then what must sub-Saharan Africa do for herself?

Basa: Abi, dat one na Compulsory Question. I lie?

Gomido: Never mind. Until sub-Saharan Africa accepts the blame for her predicament, we shall still be a long way away from a practical solution to her problems. So long as Sub-Saharan Africa produces what her children do not consume, and continues to consume what she does not produce, the sub-region and her children shall continue to be at the mercy of the developed countries.

Chaka: Can you please elaborate on that?

Gomido: You see, the case of some of the Heads of State within the Sub-Region can be likened to that of an irresponsible person who fails to lead a sensible life and gets malaria. Instead of consulting a medical doctor in his own country, who specialises in tropical medicine, what does he do? He gets on the plane, flies from one country to the other… consulting foreign brain surgeons and turning round to blame the surgeons for prescribing what they know best.

[*Basabasa and Abutu burst out laughing.*]

Chaka: Next! Yes… you at the back there. Please come forward. (Pause)

Abutu: [*With typical Nigerian-Yoruba accent*] Thank you. I am Femi Olarigbigbe. I work for the Morning Star of Nigeria and I have two questions. One, what is going to be your party's position on culture?

Basa: Dat one na compulsory question. [*To Chaka*] Abi I lie?

Gomido: That's Okay. Well, if a people have no culture, if it has no worthwhile tradition, it becomes a negligible factor in the thought of the world, and it stands in danger of being exterminated. On the basis of this assertion, we shall strive to supply the necessary inputs to the relevant institutions to ensure a vibrant and sustainable national culture.

Abutu: Question number two. What is your party's position on the regular fracas arising out of the enforcement of the ban on drumming and noise making within certain traditional areas of our land, and the refusal of some Christian churches to abide by it?

Chaka: I believe that is an optional question.

Abutu&Basa: Yes, it is optional but he may answer to earn a bonus point.

Gomido: [*Very gently*] The path crosses the stream,
              The stream crosses the path.
              Which is the elder? [*Pause*]
              The path was created by man to meet the stream. The stream has been there since creation. Even though they cross each other's path. The stream has never quarrelled with the path. They have learnt   to coexist peacefully in the bosom of nature's harmony.

Basa: [*Mimicking a woman's voice*] Ma men,
              I wan ask two question. I am Angelina Obolo, de General secretary of de West African Association of Housewives based in Liberia. An NGO. Tell me, Mr. Senator-to-be, what is your package for de plenty housewives suffering in de countryside? That is question number one.

Gomido: For us, the term Housewife shall not be part of the political lexicon. DOMESTIC ENGINEERS shall be the replacement. That, I think, is much more dignifying, even if only semantically.

Basa: Beg your pardon…Wetin be dat sementic….
            You mean you go give de housewife
            cement make dem take build house?

Abutu: No, he'll give them Cement for the
            building of gutters in your mouth.

Basa: Beg your pardon!,

Abutu: Beg your illiteracy. That is why I say go to
            school.

Chaka: [*Sternly*] Enough of that.! BASABASA,
            are you ready with your second question
            or not? Time is running.

Basa: Question number two. If you get the
            power, what policies will you put in place
            to check the wife molesters in our society?

Gomido: That's a good question. Violence against
            women. We shall introduce a new concept
            of women empowerment that shall require
            all women to be trained in martial arts
            and equipped with boxing gloves to be
            worn over their minds for mental defence.

Chaka: A sort of mind shield I suppose.

Gomido: Precisely. Much better than a Domestic
            Violence Bill that was violently dragged
            through parliament like a cow to the

abattoir.

Chaka: The last question, and I ask it. I am Nick Lancey from the BBC. African Service, London. How do you intend to help lift this dark poverty curtain off the sub-region?

Abutu &Basa: Compulsory question please!

Gomido: [*Heaves a sigh*] Let me refer you to something General Colin Powell said to me many years ago. He said, and I quote.

"The worst kind of poverty Is not economic poverty It is the poverty of sharing It is the poverty of love"unquote.
Let us therefore love one another and treat one another as human beings and not as Anglophone, Francophone, Christianphone, Muslimphone, Gramophone, Microphone, Telephone and what have you. It is only when we stop these senseless balkanisation of humanity that we shall find ourselves on the road to making life better for the people in the sub-region. Thank you and may God bless you.

[Thunderous applause from the rest]

Chaka: [*Still clapping.*] Well… well… well…
                Isn't it a shame how as a nation we cry
                for a saviour and yet lock up such brains
                behind all sorts of artificial prison bars?
                We are quick to accuse others of draining
                our best brains, but fail to see the internal
                brain drain we are carrying out very subtly
                on ourselves by the use of our prison
                systems. My brother, Gomido, note down
                my name as your Campaign Manager.

Gomido: Thank you.

Basa: Me too.

Abutu: All of us can't belong to the same political
                party. Somebody must be in opposition
                just to oppose issues. That is the beauty of
                democracy. I choose to be in the opposition.

Chaka: That's your choice. By the way, which
                constituency are you going to be standing
                for?

Abutu: Need you ask? Prison constituency of
                course.

Chaka: And the name of the party?

Abutu: P.G.P.P. of course

Basa: Beg your pardon… P.G.P.P. wetin be dat?

Abutu: Prison Graduates Popular Party.

Basa: Wetin go be de party him slogan?

Gomido: That is in the pipeline.

Basa: Too bad, by de time de slogan reach here
             ego make wet. [*General laughter.*] Why
             you dey laugh?

             [*Long General Laughter*]

[BLACK OUT]

.... **LEG 2** ....

[Cool Ghanaian higlife music. Allow it to linger in the background for a few seconds]

Abutu: Folks, we've rested enough. I suggest we get on the move.

Basa: Beg your pardon...Why?

Abutu: I don't feel too comfortable here.

Chaka: That is natural.

Abutu: What is?

Chaka: Considering the fact that you've been in prison for all these years. It is only natural you won't be comfortable with your freedom.

Basa: If de Comfort wey ino good, make una try Mercy.

Abutu: Listen to that beg-your-pardon-illiterate. As for you... you are just like a . . . a . . . a . . .

Chaka: Please... please. . . no more insults. Please
             [*Pause*]

Abutu: All right. I forgive him.

Chaka: Now, tell us what your worries are.

Abutu: This idea of living too close to a prison,
             long after you've been discharged, gives
             me the creeps.

Gomido: What do you mean?

Abutu: It is like hanging around the graveyard
             long after the cortege has gone away. It
             has its own temptations and wrongful
             interpretations.

Chaka: Explain what you mean by that.

Abutu: You see, in the case of the graveyard, we
             could be mistaken for grave looters

Basa & Chaka: What!

Gomido: Considering the way we are dressed.

Chaka: Yes, that's possible. And the other?

Abutu: We could be mistaken for escaped inmates
             and hurled back inside to do a time-added
             on.

Gomido: That is impossible.

Chaka: Never ever use the word IMPOSSIBLE
            here. This is a sub-Saharan democracy.
            Everything and anything is possible. The
            Attorney General could call for a judicial
            review of the amnesty that set us free.

Abutu: And before you can say Jack-where-
            are-you? You'd have been arrested at
            church on Sunday morning, processed
            by Monday morning and fast tracked into
            jail by Tuesday dawn.

Basa: Abi make we comot from dis place before
            wahala come take we for inside jail yard
            again. Yoo!

Gomido: My brother relax, nothing is going to
            happen to us. We have our discharge
            papers on us.

Abutu: Supposing the discharge papers turn out
            to be fake.

Basa: Walahi...somitin serious go hapin. Kai...
            I swear... Somebody go die... Allah!

Gomido: Or may be we deciding to go back into
            prison voluntarily.

Abutu: Impossible!. . . God forbid!

Basa: To go back in side? Never! Forward
         EVER! Backwards NEVER!
         [*Chaka and the others laugh*]

Chaka: Let us rather celebrate our freedom in
         song. [*Pause*] What do you say?

Abutu: I am not in a singing mood.

Chaka & Co: What at all is the matter with you?

Abutu: Folks, my stomach. I need food. I am
         hungry!

Basa: I ged am! Oh yes! I ged am. Now I sabey
         de job I want do.

Chaka: He wants to be a civil servant.

Basa: Beg your... Abi I no want to be nobody
         him servant. I be free person. I comot
         from prison. I be my own master. Free
         body!

Gomido: Then you join the IRS

Basa: IRS? Ibi some new F.M. Radio Station?

Gomido: Internal Revenue. Services. [*Enticingly*]
         That is where you make all the big bucks.
         A guy is supposed to pay a tax of twenty
         Thousand Cedis. You arrive at a gentleman's

agreement with him. He pays only twenty cedis, you enter three extra zeros as if he has paid in full and he gives you a gift of ten thousand cedis.

Basa: Dat one na bribe. . . Beg your…

Chaka: Shut up. Everyone in the civil service does it.

Basa: Na so? Me I no sabey.

Gomido: That is the lubricant that keeps the engine of the African civil service running chuku-chaka-chuku-chaka like a locomotive engine, carrying only the rich and leaving the poor behind on the tracks.

Abutu: Have you forgotten the civil servants' prayer?

Chaka & All: " …*and give us this day our daily bribe as we receive from all those whose jobs pass through our hands.*" [*General laughter*]

Basa: De Civil Service. Ibi Evil Service. I go work for Japanese restaurant.

Gomido & Co: As what?

Chaka: As the Chef, perhaps.

Basa: Not the Chef. As a Waiter.

Abutu: Why that?

Basa: Because I love am so.

Chaka: This is one thing I still can't understand about my people.

Gomido: What is it my brother?

Chaka: Why is it that we would always want to work for someone else but never for ourselves? If we are not working for a former colonial master, you can bet we are working for a former colonial master's skin-mate.

Abutu: How dare you say that? That is most unfair. You sound racist

Gomido: Forgive me, If you think I do, but that is the global fact.

Abutu: It still beats my mind though. [*Pause*]. Well, Now, you, Chaka.

Chaka: Me? What of me?

Basa: Wetin you go be, after Prison? Beg your pard. . .

Chaka: I am going to be an Abusua Panyin.

Gomido: What is that?

Basa: A traditional title. A big family head.
             Sometin like you be big chief inside small
             village.

Chaka: That's right. It is an established post in
             our traditional set up.

Abutu: What is the job description attached to
             the designation?

Chaka: Can't tell you now, but at the appropriate
             time you all shall get to know.

Gomido: Very well, that leaves you ABUTU to tell
             us how you intend celebrating your
             emancipation.

Abutu: Well, I intend to approach one of these
             foreign NGOs for assistance to enable me
             set up.

Chaka & Co: To set up what?

Abutu: My business of course.

Basa: And de name of de business? [*Laughs*]
             Beg your pardon. . .

Abutu: Ku Enye Ga Enterprise. Or Death is
             Money Enterprise.

Gomido: Dealing in what?

Abutu: Coffins and caskets.

Basa: Beg your pardon. . . why coffins and
              caskets?

Chaka: I tell you, our brother is suffering from
              Cemetery cocidiosis. [*Laughter*]

Chaka: Who gave you this silly idea that what
              society needs most is coffin and caskets?

Basa: De tin people want be food, clothing and
              roof over dem head.

Gomido: And Medicare.

**[Rummages through his bag and brings out an
old news paper.]**

Abutu: Read this. *"Over two hundred people infected
              with the deadly HIV/AIDS virus everyday
              in our land"*. What does that tell you?
              Don't be daft. What it means is that there
              is a more profitable future for coffin makers
              and gravediggers here in sub Saharan
              Africa than there is for Accountants and
              I.C.T professionals.

Gomido: I am still not convinced.

Basa: Make you prove de 'Ku-enye-ga' theory.

Chaka & Co: Yes, prove it to us that indeed Death
                brings Wealth.

Abutu: I'll do so on one condition.

Chaka: And what is that?

Abutu: That one of you is prepared to die.

Chaka & Co: What?

Basa: I beg your pardon. I no dey inside.

Gomido: Not me either. I don't want death for a
                companion.

Abutu: Cowards that you are. You desire the
                fruits of death and yet would not dare
                venture into death's orchard.

Gomido: How dare you call me a coward? Don't
                you know who I am? I am Sortorme
                Gomido Tsorgali. Great grandson of
                Torgbuiga Whuti of Wheta. The man who
                dived under water and fought two live
                crocodiles with his bare hands whilst still
                smoking a lighted pipe. I don't fear death.
                I volunteer to die. [*lies down*] Look I am
                dead!

Chaka: Yes, Gomey is dead. Look his eyes are shut.

Basa: De man die, now where de money dey?

Abutu: I am afraid that is too cheap a death to die.

Chaka & Co: Too cheap you said?

Abutu: You heard me right.

Basa: All closing eyes no be die?

Abutu: Since there is an expensive way to live,
              naturally, there ought to be an expensive
              way to die.

Chaka: So, tell us, how.

Abutu: First, you fall sick as a result of high blood
              pressure, or some Cardio Vascular Arrest
              and be rushed in a Mercedes Benz, C.
              Class, to either Nyaho Clinic or SSNIT
              Hospital.

Basa: Or Korle-Bu Teachers Hospital.

Abutu: If you don't mind medical students
              using your body as a teaching aid, then go
              to a Teaching Hospital.

Gomido: [*Pretending to be short of breath*] I prefer
              to be taken to the Military Hospital

Basa:	Beg your pardon. . . You be soldier?
Gomido:	[*Feigning severe chest pains*] Adjiiiiiiiiiiii. Mmmmmm!.. Aaaaaoooo!. . . Somebody help me!
Chaka:	What's the matter Gomey?
Gomido:	My chest! . . .Aaaaoooo! . . . the left side of my . . . Aaaaa oooo! [*Panting*] Ao God, am I really going to die?
Basa:	Abi make we carry am go throw way for hospital. Oya!
Abutu:	Let me get a taxi then.
Chaka:	With what are you going to pay for the taxi?
Abutu:	[*Gomido is groaning loudly*] [*To Chaka*] Abusua Painyin. . . please lend us some money for taxi to...
Chaka:	Me? My money, for you to take this man to the hospital. What has he ever done for me? I am sorry. I don't have a dime.
Abutu:	So what do we do? Leave him here to die because we have no cash to carry him to the hospital?

Basa: Abi make una improvise. Make una use
            una head.

Abutu: Why don't you use your back instead?

Basa: True-true, make I use my back.. Oya,
            Gomido make you come sit my back make
            I give you free ride…[*Uses his voice as an
            ambulance siren*]

            [BLACK OUT]

.... **LEG 3** ....

Basa: [*Desperation in his voice*] Auntie Nurse,
                 We go fit to see de doctor?

Nurse I: [*Saucily*] You cannot. Join the queue.

Basa: [*Politely*] Beg your pardon…Please nurse,
                 Dis one na emergency.

Nurse I: [*Flares up*] Beg your pardon, which of us
                 is trained to determine when a situation is
                 an emergency, you or I?

Basa: [*Softly*] Na you, madam. Beg your pardon.
                 . . I very sorry, Madam-Nurse. Make you
                 no vex (Pause)

Nurse I: [*Sucks her teeth loudly*] Where is your
                 card?

Basa: Ibi nyim dis.

Nurse I: National Health Insurance card, mister.
                 Not voters ID card.

Basa: We no ged am Madam.

Nurse I: Take him to the OPD.

Basa: Whosai de PWD dey.?

Nurse: I said OPD not PWD. Over there. Put him
              in that wheel chair and push him away.
              Just follow the arrow. The nurse at the
              other end will take his temperature and
              write down his history and refer him
              back to us.

Basa: Tank you Madam.
              [*Pause*]

Nurse II: Next!

Basa: Gudu morning Auntie nurse.

Nurse: Name!

Basa: BASA into Brackets Squared.

Nurse: Whose name is that?

Basa: Dat my original name madam.

Nurse II: Are you the patient?

Basa: Beg your pardon. . .

Nurse II: Are you the sick person coming to see the
              doctor?

Basa: [*With an air of self importance*] No, Madam,
             Ibi my broda here who sick. Me, I be him
             Ambulance driver. Na me, carry am. Him
             no fit to speak correct English. So, I be
             him terprator.

Nurse II: I want the patient's name.

Basa: Him name be, Kweku Nyankomago
             Menyawo-a Meyew Gomido D'Omingo.

Nurse II: What is that?

Basa: Dat one na him compound name.

Nurse II: Doesn't he have a shorter version of that
             Jaw-breaking tongue twister? Ask him.

Basa: Gomido! [*Pause*] Gomido!   You fit to
             hear me?

Gomido: Yes . . .I can. . . [*Coughs*] I can...[*Coughs*]

Basa: De madam-Nurse want sabey if say your
             compound name him ged revised standard
             version?

Gomido: [*Coughs with great difficulty*] Kweku...
             [*Coughs*] Duah... Kweku Dua...
             [*Long cough*]

Basa: [*To NURSE II*] Him revised standard

64

name na Kweku Duah. Simple.

Nurse II: Kweku…Dua…tell me, is it the Duah spelt with "H" at the end?

Basa: Gomido! you fit hear me?... Good. Your Duah, him ged "H" for him back side?

Gomido: [*Feigning great pain*] No, it has horns at the front like a cow.

Basa: Madam Nurse, Him say eno carry tail for him backside.

Nurse II: Age!

Basa: Mmm…well… make we say roughly… about 58 years old… Yes about dat.

Nurse II: I don't need you to guess. This is a hospital. We don't do *guestimations* here. We deal with facts and figures. Ask him for his real age and stop the guesswork.

Basa: Gomido! How old you be!?

Gomido: Tell her I'm old enough to be her father.

Nurse II: What was that he said?

Basa: Him say, him tink say him ged de same age plus your Papa.

Nurse II: No problem. [*Pause*] Is he married?

Basa: Of course, him ged wife plus plenty man
              and woman pikins.

Nurse: Let him answer for himself!

Basa: Gomido! . . . De Madam-Nurse ewan to
              marry you. But efear say your wife go beat
              am well-well.

Gomido: Tell her if I marry her and take her home,
              my wife will faint on account of her ugliness.
              If she wouldn't mind being a sixth
              mistress, I may consider her unsolicited
              proposal. [*BASA tries hard to suppress
              his laughter*]

Nurse II: What was that he said?

Basa: [*Stifling his laughter*] Him say . . .Him
              say . . . if na marriagement you want, he
              sorry. You are too late. Him hands already
              full.

Nurse II: God forbid! [*Spits*] Peuf!. . . See my finger?
              See this? It is a diamond ring. That should
              tell you I am somebody's missus!…okay?

Basa: Yes, madam.

Nurse II: Take your card and vanish from my sight.
              What impudence!

Basa: Tank you madam. Make you no vex
           madam. Na so de world be. Some want,
           dem no ged am. Some too gedam, dem no
           wantam.

Nurse I: …As I was saying, The doctor has gone
           to join his colleagues on the picket line to
           fight for better conditions of service. The
           following people should come for their
           cards and go home and die …

Basa: [*Almost out of breath*] Madam Nurse,
           we ged de card.

Nurse I: Let me see......Good,

Basa: We fit to see de Doctor now?

Nurse I: Not yet. Your deposit first.

Basa: Deposit… why? Dis one no be maternity
           case. My bruda is not pregnant.

Nurse I: The choice is entirely yours.

Basa: All right, how much be de deposit?

Nurse I: Only fifty dollars…U.S. or its equivalent
           in the local currency according to the
           inter bank exchange rates for the day.

Basa: Beg your pardon. . . You be Nurse or you

	be foreign exchange bureau operator?
Nurse I:	What did you just say?
Basa:	I wan ask say no reduction for de deposit?
Nurse I:	Reduction? This is a hospital . . .A Government Teaching Hospital and not a street side Market.
Basa:	Sorry, Madam-Nurse. So how much does that work up to in the local currency?
Nurse I:	Let's see. Let me get my pocket calculator… Here.
Basa:	My goodness !
Nurse I:	Hey what is that? Don't you know this is a hospital and you are not to shout?
Basa:	I sorry Madam, but de money. Whosai I for ged dat kine money? Gomido,
Gomido:	[*Feebly*] Hmmm. . .
Basa:	Where we for ged dis American dollar money?
Gomido:	Even if you write "for sale" on my body and send me to the market, with all my value-added sickness, I'll not be able to

	fetch that much.
Basa:	So, wetin we for do now, Gomido, my bruda?
Gomido:	Talk to the Abusua Panyin
Basa:	Beg your. . . Man wey no fit give you common Ghana Cedi for taxi to carry you to hospital, how he go fit to give 50 American Dollar?
Gomido:	May be we have to solicit for aid and donor support from international NGOs.
Basa:	Na true. Make we sit by the road side with cup in hand and make music. Who knows, some International Donor Agencies passing by, may be kind enough to drop in some coins .

Gomido sings a beautiful but sad song whiles Basa mimes collectecting money from the audience.]
Auntie Nurse . . Auntie Nurse…

Nurse I:	What is it?
Basa:	De money is ready.
Nurse I:	Let me have it.
Nurse I:	Good. You can transfer him unto this hospital trolley and bring him in. But

you'll have to wait here. I'll call you when the Doctor arrives.

Basa: Tank you, madam. I hear. [*Long pause*]

Nurse I: This is for you.

Basa: Tank You. Dis be de chit for de collection of de medicine?

Nurse I: No, that is for Lab. Test.

Basa: Beg your pardon. . . Lab text?

Nurse: Sure, It is the results of the tests that would assist the doctor in determining what medication to prescribe for you. You can go now.

BASA: Tank you Madam-Nurse, you be very kind woman. Gomido, lets go.

Gomido: [*Weakly*] Where are you off to again?

Basa: Wait here. I need to clear sometin wit de Madam-Nurse. [*Pause*]
Madam, just one more ting.

Nurse I: What is it again?

Basa: Dem say make we pay for de Lab. Text.

Nurse I: Of course, what do you expect?

Basa: But Madam-Nurse... I ...tink say all dat
               charge dey inside de American fifty dollar.
               I lie?

Nurse I: I am afraid you are wrong. The fifty
               dollars was for the doctor guessing which
               lab tests you probably needed to undergo.

Basa: Allahu Akbar! 50 dollars just for guess
               work?

Nurse I: Shh..shh...sh..It is not my fault.
               [*Whispers*] Cash and carry.

Basa: Cash and Carry!
               [*There is a loud scream from Gomido
               followed by a long pause*]

Basa: [*Calls out for help.*] Nurse my bruda dey
               die o. ...Nurse... Oh nurse...make una
               help ma bruda!
               Gomey...Gomey...Make you no die o,
               Gomey...
               Nurse!..nurse!....

Nurse I: Orderly...Orderly!

Voice: Yes Sister.

Nurse I: Come here quickly.

Voice: Yes, Sister! [Pause]

Nurse II:	Sister, here I am .
Nurse I:	[*With great urgency in her voice*] Hurry, help the young man over here send the patient to Ward "D." . Be quick! Go!
Orderly:	Ward "B"?
Nurse I:	I said Ward "D" ... "D" for Death. Quick . . .Be gone!
Basa:	[*Despondently*] Ao...my bruda don die finish.
	[*Silence.*]
	[Heavy breathing.]
Orderly:	Well, So, here we are. This is Ward "D".
Basa:	Beg your pardon. . . But abi dis one, na corridor.
Orderly:	Yes, but it is Ward "D"...Sideward.
Basa:	If dis na ward, whosai de hospital beds dey?
Orderly:	Hospital what? [*Laughs*] These days Hospital Wards are like Boarding Schools.

Once you are given admission, you go
to the Hospital Administrator for your
prospectus to know the items you have to buy.

Basa: So, we wey no ged prospectus, wetin we
          for do?

Orderly: You improvise.

Basa: Impro…impro… wetin?

Orderly: I'll show you. Help me pull these two
          benches to this side.

Basa: You wan put de live person for de top of
          hard wooden bench, as if say ibi cow meat
          una dey put for butcher table! Abi?

Orderly: [*Laughs*] One is a bench, but two equals a
          hospital bed.

Basa: And three benches make what?

Orderly: With or without blanket?

Basa: Blanket dey for top.

Orderly: That is what we call P.I.S. Presidential
          Initiated Suite. [*Laughs*] Look, you should
          be grateful to God that your brother has a
          double bench. I wish you could take a trip
          to the Maternity Block and see things for
          yourself.

Basa: Wetin dey dere?

Orderly: Over there both mothers and their newly
           born babies lie comfortably sleep on the
           bare cold terrazzo floor. Six newly–born
           fine babies sharing one cot. And you
           know something?

Basa: Wetin?

Orderly: They don't even complain. The babies
           and their mothers don't complain. They
           are happy. Day old babies being treated
           less than day old chicks on a poultry farm
           hatchery are happy.

Basa: Na so?

Orderly: Oh yes! They are very grateful for the
           generosity of the charitable medical
           system we operate.

Basa: I see… make I hask my broda if he wan
           make we take am go for de Maternity
           Block. Gomey!. . . Gomey… [*Pause*]
           Gomey, de orderly nurse say, if you dey
           here, you go labour in vain. So I want take
           you for Labour ward proper. Abi, you
           go go? Gomey! Gomido! Talk to me
           Gomey!.. Gomey! Gomey!

Orderly: No need shouting. He won't hear you.

Basa: Because of why?

Orderly: He's long gone.

Basa: Beg your pardon. . . Long gone for where?

Orderly: I am afraid he is… I… I mean… he is…

Basa: Oh No! Gomey why you for do dis to me?

Basa: So, what do we do now?

Orderly: Send him to the mortuary.

Basa: Whosai de mortuary dey?

Orderly: This way, please.

[Gomido is carried to the corner]

[BLACK OUT]

.... **LEG 4** ....

[Cockcrows, barking of dogs and chirping of birds to signify a new dawn.]

[Traditional dirge on flute creates a solemn atmosphere and light slowly come on.]

Chaka: Well, you are most welcome.

Abutu &Basa: Thank You, Nana.

Chaka: As the elders say, it is you who have journeyed. So, it is you who may be having a load-bearing tongue. You may unfold it.

Abutu: Nana, our presence here is in response to the call you sent out to all members of the bereaved family to meet and plan the funeral for our departed Royal.

Chaka: I am deeply touched by this show of friendship and brotherliness on your part. Once again, I say, you are all welcome.

Abutu & Basa: Thank you, Abusua Panyin .

Chaka: [*Clears his throat*] Errm...errrmm. Abutu, you shall be my Okyeame on this occasion.

Abutu: With all pleasure, Nana. Spit into my mouth that I may spit.

Chaka: Get it across to all family members who have gathered here that we have met to plan those customary rites that are necessary to conduct our departed brother safely through the portals that lead to the village of our ancestors.

Abutu: So says *Abusua Panyin*. That it was time the late Royal was found a fitting resting place and not left to freeze in a refrigerator as if he were a piece of edible carcass.

Chaka: This would mean going for the most expensive coffin on the market.

Abutu: So says Abusua Panyin, that the Royal remains should not be interred in some cheap wawa coffin.

Chaka: And I…. Abusua Panyin Chaka-Timbo! don't care how much the best golden coffin shall cost.

BASA: Nana, *Mmo ne kasa*! Well-spoken.

Abutu: The eagle that lays its eggs where no human eye can see has spoken. [*Pause*]

Basa: So, Beg your pardon. . . who go pay for de golden coffin?

Chaka: Mr. Beg-your-pardon, I am going to bear the full cost of the golden casket. And the full cost of the ten day long funeral. I have spoken!

Basa: But whosai we for ged de casket. De body still dey for inside mortuary.

Chaka: The coffin?

Basa: Yes, Nana.
           [*Abutu breaks into a long laughter*]

Abutu: No need worrying yourselves. You are right at the entrance of "Ku-Enye Ga Enterprise". Yes, gentlemen, may I please help you? [*General laughter.*]

Gomido: I think Abutu's point is well-proven.

Chaka: In fact, proven beyond all reasonable doubt.

[Sudden loud thunderclaps mixed with strong blowing wind]

Abutu: Folks, we have to hurry out of here. The weather is changing.

Basa: Na true-true. Emake like ego rain.

[More thunderclap]

Chaka: I think so too. Let's look for a hiding place
                before we are soaked to our underwears.

Abutu: Let us simply get out of here.

Gomido: Out of here to where?

Abutu: To somewhere… anywhere…Just
                somewhere we can get some shelter and…

Basa: And Food!... Food! Some of we de
                hungry.

Gomido: So where do we go? [**Silence**] Are you
                all quiet? We want to move. Someone
                suggest where we should be heading from
                here. [*Pause*] Well, may be, we go back to
                the palace.

Basa: Palace…which palace be dat?

Chaka: What a question. Don't you know who
                you are? You are Princes...

Basa &Abutu: Princes?

Chaka: Yes, Royals!

Basa &Abutu: Royals?

Chaka: You are a peculiar people. A chosen
                generation. A generation belonging to
                the Palace Reserved for Important Sons
                of the Nation. [Pause] Check out the

acronym.

Basa: Wetin be acronym… beg your pardon. . .
           idey like crayon?

Abutu: No, it is an abbreviation consisting of
            letters that form a word.

Basa: Now you complicate everything for me.
           Beg your Pardon!
           [*Laughter*]

[Gentle rain drops on tin roof]

Chaka: [*Spells it*] P…R…. I…S…. O…N. stands
           for, Palace Reserved for Important Sons
           of the Nation.

Abutu: [*Vehemently*] Back to Prison? No way.
           You'll need a bulldozer and a forklift to
           carry me from here back to prison. In
           fact, you shall need a helicopter to fly me
           over these walls.

Basa: Ma bruda, why you dey shout-shout so?
           Look de time enack, by now dem dey
           serve prison ration.. . Food! . ..

Gomido: Yes, that is true. We can be sure of getting
           some warm second-hand clothes in there,

Abutu: Who needs second-hand clothes?

Gomido: At least that is better than nothing,
            considering the way we are shivering. In
            Prison, we shall become assets of the State
            and receive free medical attention.

Basa: Cash and carry go be history.

Gomido: Exactly. We shall have free shelter in
            Prison.

Abutu: Stop It... Stop it,

Basa: No rent, no Land lord coming to harass
            we.

Abutu: I say stop it! [*Silence*]

Chaka: We are in a democracy. Let us put it to
            vote. [*Pause*] Those IN favour of going
            back into the Palace Reserved for
            Important Sons of the Nation, say "Aye"!

Gomido & Basa: Aye!

Chaka: Those OUT of favour say "Nay"!

Abutu: Nay!... Nay ...and Nay! a thousand times.

Chaka: One abstention, which is I. A two-to-one
            decision. I think the Ayes have it.

Basa: Make we go quick-quick. Abi, I hungry
            too much. Make we go. By now dem dey

share de ration for insai.

[The rain intensifies.]

Gomido: Yes. It is far better in there, where we won't catch pneumonia in a society that practices Cash and Carry medical system without a human face. Let's go.

Abutu: I am a free man. I am heading for Canaan. I am never going back to Egypt.

Basa: We no dey go to Egypt. Dat place na too far. We dey go for de PALACE jus over dere. Oya, Forward NEVER, Backward EVER! Make we go now. As for me I dey hungry. Let me begin to pack our belongings for the trip back to the palace.

Chaka: Abutu, for the very last time, are you sure you are not coming along with us back into the palace?

Abutu: My mind is made up. I am determined to stay out of your so-called PALACE by every means possible.

Gomido: The rains will beat you.

Basa: Cold go catch your body and hungry go catch your belly.

Abutu: The rains will come. The cold, the hunger and even the pain may come, but they are mere circumstances that cannot hurt me forever. They all shall pass. I shall hang on outside here and set up my coffin and casket business. With 200 people being infected with the HIV/AIDS virus a daily, very soon I shall be experiencing a boom In my business. I am off.   [*Exit ABUTU*]

Chaka: Good luck then.

Gomido & Basa: Bye-bye…We're off to dine in the Palace… Bye-bye!

           [*SILENCE*]

Voice: Who is there?

Chaka & Co: [*Shivering voice*] It is we.

Voice: You, who?

Chaka & Co: We were once members of this Royal family.

Chaka: We belonged to this palace.

Voice: Your Palace IDs, please.

Chaka: I am Royal PT 007.

Voice: Yes, you were here for murder.

Gomido: That is correct. I am Royal number www
            dot 96.

Voice: You were sent here for engaging in cyber
            fraud.

Gomido: Well, something like that.

Basa: I be Royal KW66.

Voice: You were sent in here for stealing
            electrical cables meant to supply several
            kilowatts of power to 66 rural communities.

Basa: Ibi so dem put for de charge sheet.

Voice: And your mission here this evening?

Chaka & Co: We have come to re-register. Sah!

Voice: Re-register for what?

Gomido: For re-admission into the fraternity of the
            PALACE as prodigal Royals. Sah!

Voice: [*Laughter*] Why?

Basa: [*In a whisper*] Abi, make you tellam say

            we be HIPEC, Hungrily Indebted Poor
            Ex-Cons. Tell am dat. Abi, I say tellam
            quick-quick! Beg your pardon. . .

Chaka: We have not been able to handle effectively the freedom we gained from you. Sah!

Gomido: That's a lie and you know it. Rather, it was the freedom that couldn't handle us. Sah!

Voice: [*Rustic laughter*] I am afraid you are all suffering from an acute form of Acquired Prison Traumatic Syndrome. The health of other inmates could be jeopardised if you are allowed in. But first, wait and let me discuss it with my Commandant. We might have to quarantine you for a few months if you don't mind,

Basa & Co: We don't mind at all.

Gomido: Once we'll be given free meals during the period of quarantine, that's okay.

Voice: But I need to clear it first with my superior officer. Wait for me, I'll be right back.

[Shutting of Peephole. Silence]

BASA: (Earnestly) Make we pray.

Gomido & Co: [*Praying in earnest*] We lift up our eyes unto the prison… From where cometh our help!… Our help Cometh from the lord who made the prisons and its officers… He'll not suffer our stomach to go hungry. Behold........

[Sound of heavy metal gates being opened.]

[Sound of marching military boots.]

Voice: Halt!

[Sound of feet in military boots coming to sudden attention.]

Voice: I am the new Chief Prison Officer assigned to escort you inside. Here are kneepads you are to wear on your knees as you crawl back into the palace. And you shall remain confined in solitary on your knees, till the Commandant is satisfied you are completely cured of the Acquired Prison Traumatic Syndrome you are suffering from.

Chaka: Please, Officer, may I . . .

Voice: You may not. Get down on your knees, NOW!. By the left quick march. Left right... left-right... left-right.. . . Open the gates!

Abutu & Chaka: Please allow us to walk upright on our own two feet.

Voice: Too late. You forfeited that right by applying for readmission into the palace.

Printed in the United States
By Bookmasters